young men

Ken Moser

10 Publishing
a division of 10 of those.com

Published in 2013 by 10Publishing, a division of 10ofthose.com

9D Centurion Court, Farington, Leyland PR25 3UQ, England.

Email: info@10ofthose.com Website: www.10ofthose.com

ISBN 978-1-909611-43-6

Printed in the UK

young men:
contents

leader's notes available through
www.effectiveyouthministry.com

YOUNG MEN:
INTRODUCTION

Welcome to Studies for Young Men!

"Flee the evil desires of youth, and pursue righteousness, faith, love and peace, along with those who call on the Lord out of a pure heart." 2 Timothy 2:22

Being a Christian young man can be tough these days. There are so many things that can make it difficult to live a life that honors God. You want to follow Jesus, but there are so many distractions! Is it possible to be a young man and still live a life that glorifies Jesus?

Yes it is! However, it is very important that you equip yourself with teaching from God's Word. This will help you deal with the struggles you go through and assist you in the tough decisions you face each day.

Over the next six weeks you will learn what God has to say on issues like girls, the internet, bad language, fighting and being aggressive. There is even a bonus study on how to drive an automobile in a way that pleases the Lord.

My hope and prayer is that with the help of God's word, you can "flee the evil desires of youth" and "pursue" the things that God loves.

Press on brothers!

Ken Moser

Young Men:

Flee! Pursue!

Flee the evil desires of youth, and pursue righteousness, faith, love and peace, along with those who c on the Lord out of a pure heart. 2 Timothy 2:

let's get started

let's get started

1. I am looking forward to...

- [ ] getting my driver's license
- [ ] leaving school
- [ ] getting married
- [ ] travel
- [ ] having kids
- [ ] going to work (career)
- [ ] all of the above
- [ ] something else?

2. What are some things you like about being "young"?

3. What are some things you find frustrating?

going deeper

A word to young men: **2 Timothy 2:22.**

"Flee the evil desires of youth"

What does it mean to "flee the evil desires of youth"?

What are the evil desires that many people your age struggle with?

Is it possible for you to win this struggle?

How do you rate when it comes to "fleeing evil"?

1 -- 10

Bad as bad can be — Trying hard — Evil? I'm an angel!

"and pursue righteousness, faith, love, peace"

What does it mean to pursue

a) Righteousness? ______________________

b) Faith? ______________________

c) Love? ______________________

d) Peace? ______________________

In the boxes below write out a definition of the word and an idea or two that would help you to pursue it successfully. If there is time, look up a Bible verse or two.

	Definition	Helpful ideas to pursue it successfully	Helpful Bible verses
Righteousness			Matt. 5:6; Phil. 3:8-9; 2Tim. 3:16
Faith			Heb. 11:1-3; Rom. 1:17; 2Cor. 5:7; Gal. 2:20
Love			Rom. 12:9-10; 1Cor. 13:4-7; Eph. 4:2
Peace			Matt. 5:9; Col. 3:15

"along with those who call on the Lord out of a pure heart"

Why is it so important to be with people who "call on the Lord out of a pure heart"?

What does this mean for us week by week?

What do you think will happen to us if we don't meet regularly with others who call on the Lord?

Is there anything we need to change in our lives because it keeps us from meeting with others regularly?

Think Spot: **If there is time, read Hebrews 3:12-13.** What does this tell us about the importance of meeting with other Christians? How does it relate to the passage in 2 Timothy? What does it tell us about meeting together?

getting active

Helping each other

Are there things that we need to flee from and pursue this week?

How can this group help each other to do this successfully?

let's pray

- Pray that we will flee evil.
- Pray that we will pursue righteousness, faith, love and peace.
- Pray that we will gather regularly with others who have a pure heart.
- *Other things we can pray for*

Stay tuned Next week we will look at dealing with the opposite sex!

For your eyes only: The week ahead

For your eyes only:
The Week ahead

1. Personal Bible Reading

This week try to read the first six chapters of the book of Daniel. This Old Testamen book is filled with great stories about some young men who trusted in the Lord eve when everyone else around them didn't.

My Weekly Bible reading plan!

In Daniel I read (place a ✔ when you have read it!)

Chapter 1 ☐ Chapter 2 ☐ Chapter 3 ☐

Chapter 4 ☐ Chapter 5 ☐ Chapter 6 ☐

Fleeing darkness, living in the light!

Spend a moment or two and read Ephesians 4:17-5:21. In this part of the Bible we are encouraged to avoid all types of evil and live for Christ. In a way, it is a longer version of 2 Tim. 2:22. As you read it, you may want to pause and ask God to help you to put into practice all that you are reading.

(1 Timothy 6:11 is also another excellent verse that is just like the one you looked at in your small group. If you have time look it up!)

2. Memory Verse

Can you learn the memory verse at the top of the study (2 Timothy 2:22)? Give it a try this week.

Flee the evil desires of youth, and pursue righteousness, faith, love and peace, along with those who call on the Lord out of a pure heart.

2 Timothy 2:22

3. Prayer

Pray that you will live out the verse from this week's study.
Pray that you will flee any evil desires that you may have.
Pray that you will be characterized by righteousness, faith, love and peace.
Pray that this will happen in the lives of your Christian friends as well.

Things that I can thank God for: ____________________

____

____

____

____

Things that I need to ask God to help me with: ____________________

____

____

____

Young Men:
Girls

Put to death, therefore, whatever belongs to your earthly nature: sexual immorality, impurity, lust, e desires and greed, which is idolatry. Because of these, the wrath of God is coming. Colossians 3:5

let's get started

let's get started

Describe your attitude towards the opposite sex:

- ◯ Girls, what are they?
- ◯ Never think about them
- ◯ Can't stop thinking about them
- ◯ I'd give anything to have girlfriend
- ◯ Who cares. I'd rather play video games!
- ◯ Other? ____________

The Story of John (Have someone in the group read this story out loud)

John is from a Christian family and really wants to live to please God. However, he has discovered lately that he can't keep his mind off the opposite sex. He thinks about the girls in his class and the girls in his youth group. Quite often his mind wanders off and he thinks about girls in a way he knows God isn't happy with. He prays and asks God to take these thoughts away but it is still a struggle. He also wants to have a girlfriend, although he isn't sure if it is for all the right reasons. **What would you tell John?**

Just get used to it

Join a monastery

Tell his parents

Take a cold shower whenever this happens

Pray and seek help

Something else?

You'll soon grow out of it

Treating girls the way God wants us to!
Read 1 Timothy 5:1-2 (esp. v. 2).
What do you think it means to "treat younger women as sisters, with absolute purity"?

Can you give practical examples?

Are you doing this now?

Is there anything you need to change in the way you treat girls?

Lust must die! Read Colossians 3: 5-6.
(Lust– an intense craving or desire. It is often associated with sex.)
What practical things can you do to put lust "to death"?

What do these verses tell us will happen to those who live according to their sinful desires?

think spot: **Dealing with impure thoughts- one man's solution!**
Read Job 31:1.

How was Job (pronounced Jobe) able to do this?

Is this something any guy can do?

What are some practical things you can do to stop looking lustfully at the opposite sex?

Don't mess up with the girls in your youth group!

Read Ephesians 5:3-7.

Write down what we must not have in our youth group (you should find si things)

1) ____________ 2) ____________ 3) ____________

4) ____________ 5) ____________ 6) ____________

What happens to those who are "disobedient" according to v.6?

According to v. 5, what don't they have?

How can we live out this part of the Bible- is it possible? (What things do w need to do and not do?)

How do we pursue good friendships with the opposite sex, yet stay away fror doing things that dishonor Jesus?

getting active

Helping each other

In light of what we have read today do you have any advice for John (he's the guy we read about at the beginning of our study)?

Is there anything that needs to change in your life as a result of today's study?

Can we make a promise to each other to discourage lust and immorality in this group?

let's pray

- Pray that we can put into practice what we have learned from God's Word today.
- Pray that each person in the group will treat girls with absolute purity.
- Pray for strength to avoid temptation and lust.
- *Other things we can pray for* ____________________

____

____

stay tuned

Next week we will look at honoring God and surfing the Internet!

For your eyes only:
The week ahead

For your eyes only:
The week ahead

1. Personal Bible Reading

Did you read first six chapters of the book of Daniel? Let's move on and read thre chapters from the Old Testament book of Judges. Here you will read about a youn man named Gideon. Read Judges 6:1-8:35. Read a bit of this each day. (If you didn finish Daniel 1-6, finish this week.)

My weekly Bible reading plan!

In Judges I read (place a ✔ when you have read it!)

Chapter 6 ☐ Chapter 7 ☐ Chapter 8 ☐

Finding a girlfriend & (later on) a wife!

The Bible has a lot to say about what kind of woman you should pursue. Read Proverbs 31:10-31 and think through what this excellent passage of the Bible is saying to us about who we should marry. After this, read 1 Corinthians 7 (the whole chapter). This chapter is full of good advice about going out and getting married. You may want to read through it a few times.

After reading these passages from the Bible:

What should we look for in the opposite sex? What things should we avoid?

Is it necessary to have a girlfriend (or get married)? What about those who are single, what does God think about them?

2. Memory Verse

Can you learn the memory verse at the top of the study (Colossians 3:5-6)? Give it a try this week.

Put to death, therefore, whatever belongs to your earthly nature: sexual immorality, impurity, lust, evil desires and greed, which is idolatry. Because of these, the wrath of God is coming.

Colossians 3:5-6

3. Prayer

Pray that you will treat the opposite sex well.
Pray that you will fight lustful thoughts and inappropriate behavior.
Pray that this will happen in the lives of your Christian friends as well.

Things that I can thank God for: ____________________

Things that I need to ask God to help me with: ____________________

Young Men: Honoring Jesus on the Internet!

Finally, brothers, whatever is true, whatever is noble, whatever is right, whatever is pure, whatever is lo whatever is admirable — if anything is excellent or praiseworthy — think about such things. Philippians

let's get started

How much time do you spend on the Internet? (Circle your answer)

- *Every waking minute!*
- *About an hour a day*
- *Every now and then*
- *Only when my parents let me*
- *Never- I'm too busy outside playing sports*
- *Other* ______________

The Story of Greg (Have someone in the group read this story out loud)

Greg is 15 years old and a Christian. Lately he realizes that he can't stop thinking about the opposite sex. He finds himself daydreaming about them too many times a day to count! It has gotten much worse now that he has his own computer. It is in his room and it is connected to the internet. He has now entered into a whole new world of lust. He finds himself going to websites and looking at things that he knows he shouldn't. He knows what he is doing is wrong and that he needs help, yet he is too ashamed to speak to anyone about it. **What is your advice for Greg? How could you help him as a Christian brother?**

Review

Can anyone remember Job 31:1 from our last study? (Look it up again if you can't remember.) What does this say to us about the temptations we face surfing the Internet?

going deeper

going deeper

God takes sin very seriously! **Read Matthew 18:7-9.**
What clear instruction is Jesus giving here?

How are we to respond to it?

Why is Jesus is so strong in his condemnation of sin?

We must avoid doing what non-Christians sometimes do.
Read Ephesians 4:17-19. (FYI: The Bible sometimes calls non-Christians "Gentiles")
According to this passage, why do non-Christians do evil?

How are we to be different?

How do we relate this teaching to the Internet?

Keep your mind focused on good things. **Read Philippians 4:8.**
Can you give examples of a few of the eight things we are to think about?

What can we do to make sure we keep our minds on good things and avoid thoughts that can lead us into sin? Give some practical examples.

think spot: **In the near future...**

A friend tells you that his parents are going away for the weekend and invites you over to look at Internet porn with some other friends. If you say "no", he will tell his friends and they will think you are a loser. If you go, you will watch something that you know you shouldn't and the images will continue to make it hard for you to keep your thoughts pure long after you have watched it. **What do you do?**

- ○ Lie to him and tell him you're busy
- ○ Say "yes" because you want to be accepted
- ○ Tell him you'll get back to him later
- ○ Send him a computer virus to crash his computer
- ○ Tell him "no way" and forget about the ramifications
- ○ Find new friends
- ○ Have your dad challenge his dad to a fight
- ○ Something else? ______________________

getting active

Helping each other

In light of what we have read today, do you have any advice for Greg? (He's the guy we read about at the beginning of our study.)

What can we do this week to make sure we honor Jesus with our computers?

let's pray

- Pray that we will intentionally avoid unhelpful images on the Internet (and in DVDs).
- Pray that we will all have strength to keep our minds on good things.
- Pray for anyone who is struggling with this issue.
- *Other things we can pray for* ______________________________

____

stay tuned

Next week we will look at what the Bible has to say about the way we speak!

For your eyes only:
The week ahead

For your eyes only:
The Week ahead

1. Personal Bible Reading

Did you enjoy reading about Gideon? It is time to move on to another famous person in the book of Judges. He is the great "Samson". While he was a great man of God he also had his weaknesses and struggles. This week read Judges chapters 13-16. You will see that in the end he was a man who wanted to serve the Lord. (Samson is listed as one of the "heroes of the faith" in Hebrews 11:32-38.

My weekly Bible reading plan!

In Judges I read (place a ✔ when you have read it!)

Chapter 13 ☐ Chapter 14 ☐ Chapter 15 ☐ Chapter 16 ☐

2. Memory Verse

Can you learn the memory verse at the top of the study (Phil. 4:8)? Give it a try this week.

Finally, brothers, whatever is true, whatever is noble, whatever is right, whatever is pure, whatever is lovely, whatever is admirable — if anything is excellent or praiseworthy — think about such things.

Philippians 4:8

Pray that you will continue to honor Jesus as you surf the net.

Pray that you will avoid unhelpful websites and DVDs.

Keep praying for your friends as well.

Things that I can thank God for: ______________________

____

____

Things that I need to ask God to help me with: ______________________

____

____

Hot tips for keeping your computer a friend rather than an enemy!

If you are finding the Internet a struggle, here are a number of things you can do to surf the net and honor Jesus at the same time!

1. Keep your computer in a more public place than your bedroom. In other words, don't have access to the Internet in a place where you can lock the doors and be alone.
2. Buy some software that will lock out unhelpful sites and let someone else set the password.
3. Have a buddy that you can be honest with. This person will pray for you and check every now and then to see how you're going. This is a hard thing to do at first but in the end it will help to keep you out of trouble.
4. When you feel the temptation to go to unhelpful sites, you need to pray and ask for God's help. In addition to this, leave your computer straight away and do something else.
5. Remember what we learnt in study 2; that God wants us to treat the opposite sex with respect. It is also important to keep in mind what study 1 taught us to do when faced with temptation: don't believe the lie; flee!
6. When you fail, you need to remember that God forgives all those who come to him in repentance. Read 1 John 1:8-2:2 (and Psalm 32 & 51!). Tell God that you are sorry, and that you will really try to avoid this in the future and thank Him for Jesus' death on the cross to bring forgiveness.
7. One of the best ways to avoid bad sites on the net is to never begin in the first place. If you haven't yet fallen into this trap- say a quiet prayer of thanks and stay away!

Young Men: Language (joking, swearing, harsh words, etc.)

Do not let any unwholesome talk come out of your mouths, but only what is helpful for buildin[g] others up according to their needs, that it may benefit those who listen. Ephesians 4:29 1:

let's get started

let's get started

1 When it comes to the way I speak … (circle your answer)

I have a mouth like a sewer! (I really struggle with this issue)

I only say bad things when my computer crashes

Occasionally I fall, but I try not to!

I never say bad things (I'm an angel)

2 I mainly have trouble with swearing (place a ✔ in the box)

- ☐ when I'm alone
- ☐ with my non-Christian friends
- ☐ all the time!
- ☐ never
- ☐ on the sporting field
- ☐ when things go wrong
- ☐ rarely
- ☐ other ______________________

The Story of Tim (Have someone in the group read this story out loud)

Tim hangs around a group of guys at school who speak in a way that clearly doesn't honor God They tell rough jokes, swear a lot and are always saying "oh-my-gawd" and "jeezus christ". In addition to this, they often make jokes at each other's expense and put each other down. Tim struggles with this and sometimes even joins in. While he's not happy with this, he puts up with it, since they are his only friends at school. **What advice would you give Tim?**

- ○ time to get new friends ○ cry
- ○ punch them every time they say something bad
- ○ have a deep chat with them about the issue ○ ignore it
- ○ if you can't beat 'em, join 'em ○ other ________________

going deeper

going deeper

Be careful what comes out of your mouth! **Read Colossians 3:8-10 (You may want to read v.5-7 as well).**

What does it mean to "slander" someone? Why do you think God hates it?

Is it possible for us to get rid of "filthy language"? What do we need to do every day to remove it from the way we speak?

What about lying, is it possible not to lie? Why do you think God loves honesty? (If you want more on lying, turn to Eph. 4:25.)

We must use words that "build up". **Read Ephesians 4:29.**

What do you think "unwholesome talk" means? Can you give examples?

What type of speech are we to replace it with? Why?

How does this group rate when it comes to "building each other up" in the way we speak to each other? How can we improve?

think spot: 1 The 3rd Commandment- God is not a swear word! Exodus 20:7.

What does this commandment clearly tell us?

Why do you think God hates having his name misused?

How can you avoid doing this?

What can you do if all your friends continually break this commandment?

think spot: 2 The great name of Jesus Christ! Acts 4:8-12.

(In the previous chapter we read that Peter and John healed a lame man "in the name of Jesus Christ". After this, Peter and John preached to the crowd and were thrown in jail!)

What does this passage say about who Jesus Christ is?

What does v. 12 tell us about his importance?

In light of this, why is it wrong to use his name as a swear word?

How could we explain to our non-Christian friends that it is offensive to God and to us to hear His name used as a swear word?

If you want to read more about how great Jesus is, read Acts 10:34-43 and Col. 1:15-20.

getting active

getting active

Helping each other

In light of what we have read today, do you have any advice for Tim? (He's the guy we read about at the beginning of our study.)

What can we do to help each other honor God in our speech?

Is there anything that we need to change in light of today's study?

let's pray

- Pray that we will speak in a way that honors God.
- Pray that we will get rid of bad habits and unwholesome talk.
- Pray that we will have strength to encourage our friends to change the way they speak (if this is needed)!
- *Other things we can pray for* ______________________

stay tuned Next week we will look at honoring God by not fighting!

For your eyes only:
The week ahead

For your eyes only:

The Week ahead

1. Personal Bible Reading

Did you find time to read about Samson? This week we will move to the Old Testame[nt] book of 1 Samuel where we will read about Samuel. He was a great man who serve[d] God all his life. Read chapters 1-4.

My Weekly Bible reading plan!

In Samuel I read (place a ✔ when you have read it!)

Chapter 1 ☐ Chapter 2 ☐ Chapter 3 ☐ Chapter 4 ☐

2. Memory Verse

Can you learn the memory verse at the start of the study (1 John 1:9)? Give it a try this week.

Do not let any unwholesome talk come out of your mouths, but only what is helpful for building others up according to their needs, that it may benefit those who listen.

Ephesians 4:29

3. Prayer

Pray that you will live out this week's study.

Pray that you will be characterized by speech that honors God.

Pray that this will happen in the lives of your Christian friends as well.

Pray for anything in particular that you struggle with.

Things that I can thank God for: ____________________

Things that I need to ask God to help me with: ____________________

Be careful: our words are powerful things!

You have probably said something that you later regretted. You have no doubt also had someone say something to you that really hurt. The Bible warns us that our speech is something that can be used for good and for bad!

Read James 3:3-12.

List 5 things James says about the tongue:

How can you be wiser with the use of your tongue?

How can you learn to use the tongue for good?

Young Men: Being Peaceful in an Aggressive World!

Blessed are the peacemakers, for they will be called sons of God. Matthew 5

let's get started

I would describe myself as…

- ☐ mellow ("I'm a lover, not a fighter")
- ☐ I only get aggressive when pushed
- ☐ I'm feisty a lot of the time
- ☐ I'm a walking time bomb- look at me and I explode
- ☐ Something else? ____________________

The Story of Drew (Have someone in the group read this story out loud)

Drew has a close group of friends at school. However, there is another group in his school that they don't get along with. Usually they just say things to each other and give each other dirty looks. Lately, though, it is getting more heated. It looks as if there may even be a fight between a couple of the guys from each group. **What should Drew do? What could he do to bring peace between the two groups? What should he do if there actually is a fight?**

The Book of Proverbs
Have each member of the group look up one of these proverbs and read them to the group. Briefly discuss what each of them teaches us.

15:18 17:1 17:14 20:3 26:17

What things can you do to avoid quarrels? Give some practical examples.

1.

2.

3.

God loves those who make peace! **Read Matthew 5:9.**
What is the promise given here to someone who is a peacemaker?

Do you consider yourself to be a peacemaker?

Are you characterized by peace at school? At home? At work? On the sporting field? At parties?

God wants us to be self-controlled. **Read Titus 2:6.**
What do you think it means to be "self-controlled"?

How does this relate to fighting and being aggressive?

How can we be more self-controlled with people and situations that make us angry?

Do you have trouble being patient (and peaceful) with any of the following people? (Place a ✔ next to your answers)

- ○ My sister/brother
- ○ My parents
- ○ My teacher(s)
- ○ My old girlfriend
- ○ Some of the kids in the youth group
- ○ People at my school
- ○ People I compete against in sports
- ○ Other? ____________

think spot: Helpful hints from the word of God

The Bible is full of helpful hints to avoid strife and conflict. **Read Matthew 6:14-15.** What does this passage tell us to do? Do you find this easy to do? Why? Why not?

Read Ephesians 4:31-32. What does this passage tell us to do? How will this help us avoid fights?

Read Philippians 2:14-15. What can you do to avoid complaining or arguing this week?

getting active

getting active

Helping each other

In light of what we have read today, what advice would you give Drew (he's the guy we read about earlier)?

How can we help each other to be peaceful and not fight?

What can we do to be more self-controlled?

let's pray

- Pray that we will be self-controlled and peaceful.
- Pray that we will avoid quarrels and fights.
- *Other things we can pray for*

____

____

stay tuned

Next week we will have another great Bible study together!

For your eyes only:
The week ahead

For your eyes only:

The Week ahead

1. Personal Bible Reading

This week let's keep reading about some of the great men of the past. It is now tin to read about Solomon. Read 1 Kings 1-4 and learn about one of the wisest m who ever lived (see 4:29-34)! [If you want to read more from God's word on living peace, read Colossians 3:12-15 & James 4:1-12.]

My weekly Bible reading plan!

In 1 Kings I read (place a ✔ when you have read it!)

Chapter 1 ☐ Chapter 2 ☐ Chapter 3 ☐ Chapter 4 ☐

2. Memory Verse

Can you learn the memory verse at the top of the study (Matt. 5:9)? Give it a try th week.

Blessed are the peacemakers, for they will be called sons of God.

Matthew 5:9

3. Prayer

Pray that you will live out this week's study.

Pray that you will be characterized by peace.

Pray that this will happen in the lives of your Christian friends as well.

Things that I can thank God for: ______________________________

____

____

Things that I need to ask God to help me with: ______________________________

____

____

Hot tips to avoid a fight:

There are a number of things we all must learn to do to avoid conflict. Here's a brief list:

1. Learn to listen. Sometimes a fight happens merely because of a miscommunication.
2. Learn to say "sorry". If you have wronged someone else, swallow your pride and apologize.
3. Slow down, take a breath and try not to respond immediately with anger. Ask for God to give you patience and wisdom before you react to a situation.
4. Learn to forgive when somebody does something that hurts you. Remember Matthew 6:14-15!
5. Never resort to physical violence unless you or someone else's is being threatened.
6. If you have a conflict with someone, find a person who can mediate and bring peace.
7. If you find yourself getting upset over a little thing, try to remember that it is a little thing. Don't blow things out of proportion.
8. Pray for the fruits of the Spirit: patience, gentleness, self-control, etc. (Galatians 5:22-23.)
9. Finally, choose your friends carefully. Friends who are aggressive and fight will no doubt have an influence on you.

Young Men: Driving!

And whatever you do, whether in word or deed, do it all in the name of the Lord Jes
giving thanks to God the Father through him. Colossians 3

let's get started

let's get started

Have you ever thought you were going to be in a car accident? What was the situation? How did you feel?

1 In most cities, car accidents are the most common way for young men to die. How do you feel when you hear this?

- ◯ It won't happen to me!
- ◯ I'll slow down for a while and then drive like a maniac again
- ◯ I'm a good driver- I can handle a car
- ◯ I'm going to drive like grandpa after hearing this!
- ◯ Something else? ______________

2 Why is it so tough to tell your friends not to drive too fast?

going deeper

The Bible doesn't say a lot about automobiles (they usually walked back then!). However, there are some guidelines that we can follow.

Obey the law: Part 1! **Read Romans 13:1-5.**
What does this say about obeying the law?

____

____

Why is so tough to obey the law when we're driving?

How can we do a better job?

Obey the law: Part 2! **Read Titus 3:1.**
How does this relate to being in a car?

____

____

How should we act when we drive together?

What happens if a passenger urges us to drive too fast or to drive recklessly?

Glorify God in everything you do! **Read Colossians 3:17.**
What does this verse tell us about how we should live?

____

____

How can we relate this to being in a car?

Helping each other

How can this group honor Jesus in the way we drive?

How can we help each other to drive safely?

think spot: 1 You're a passenger with a "crazy driver"!

What should you do if you get into the car with a driver who turns out to be a crazy driver?

- ◯ Grab the wheel and say, "I'm driving"
- ◯ Don't get in until you quiz them thoroughly
- ◯ Lie about your destination and get out early
- ◯ Immediately talk to them about the way they are driving
- ◯ Close your eyes and think of a happy place
- ◯ Pray out loud
- ◯ Something else? ____________________

think spot: 2 What about aggressive driving & road rage?

Why do some people seem to be so angry and aggressive when driving? How can we stay calm when driving? Can you list 3 things that you can do to avoid getting cranky behind the wheel? What should you do if an aggressive driver confronts you on the road?

let's pray

- Pray that we can drive in a responsible way that honors Jesus.
- Pray that no one in this group will ever be harmed in an automobile accident.
- *Other things we can pray for*

____

____

____

For your eyes only:
The week ahead

thank you

Thanks to Belinda Hopper and Susie Ley for their proofreading editing.
Thanks also to Sarah van Delden for her work on the layout and graphics.

Other recommended resources for your youth ministry:

Small Group Bible Studies

Starting Out
By Ken Moser

Foundations For Christian Living
By Ken Moser

Young Women
By Julie Moser

Luke: Who is Jesus?
By Ken Moser

Luke: Jesus' Parables
By Ken Moser

Luke: Carry Your Cross
By Ken Moser

Death And Resurrection Of Jesus
By Julie Moser

Work Rest Play
By Ken Moser

Big Issues For Today's Youth
By Ken Moser

Studies 2 Go
By Julie Moser

More Studies 2 Go
By Julie Moser

Resources for Leaders

Programs 2 Go
By Ken Moser

Changing the World through Effective Youth Ministry
By Ken Moser

Creative Christian Ideas for Youth Groups
By Ken Moser

Youth Evangelism: Reaching Young People in a Way that Honours God
By Ken Moser